An Address Upon The Forests Of New Hampshire

Joseph Burbeen Walker

In the interest of creating a more extensive selection of rare historical book reprints, we have chosen to reproduce this title even though it may possibly have occasional imperfections such as missing and blurred pages, missing text, poor pictures, markings, dark backgrounds and other reproduction issues beyond our control. Because this work is culturally important, we have made it available as a part of our commitment to protecting, preserving and promoting the world's literature. Thank you for your understanding.

AN ADDRESS

UPON THE

FORESTS OF NEW HAMPSHIRE,

BY

JOSEPH B. WALKER.

DELIVERED BEFORE SEVERAL MEETINGS HELD UNDER THE
AUSPICES OF THE BOARD OF AGRICULTURE, DURING
THE WINTER OF 1871-72.

MANCHESTER:
CAMPBELL & HANSCOM, PRINTERS, 839 ELM STREET.
1872.

OUR FORESTS.

[An Address delivered at various Farmers' Meetings, by JOSEPH B. WALKER of Concord.]

You may all, perhaps, remember the sage advice of the dying Laird of Dumbiedikes to Jock, his by no means hopeful son and heir, "Jock, when ye hae naething else to do, ye may be aye sticking in a tree; it will be growing, Jock, while ye're sleeping." Although Jock, in his stupidity, appreciated little this good counsel of his father, it may be well for us to take a hint from it and bethink ourselves, more than we have been wont to do, of our wood and timber lands.

THEIR IMPORTANCE.

We are in little danger of exaggerating their importance. Of the nearly six millions of acres, (5,930,200,) constituting the area of New Hampshire, probably about three millions, or one-half of the whole number, are covered with forests.* These, some of very recent and some of primeval growth, not confined to any one section, are scattered over all parts of the State, in tracts varying in extent from a very few to thousands of acres. The trees of these forests are of numerous varieties, and most of them of high value for wood and timber. We find among them three distinct species of the Pine: (1) the *White Pine* (Pinus strobus); (2) the *Pitch-pine* (P. rigida); (3) the *Norway Pine* (P. resinosa).

At least six of the Oak: (1) the *White Oak* (Quercus alba); (2) the *Red Oak* (Q. rubra); (3) the *Yellow Oak* (Q. tinctoria); (4) the *Rock Chestnut Oak* (Q. montana); (5) the *Scrub Oak* (Q. ilicifolia); (6) the *Gray Oak* (Q. ambigua).

---

* The Census of 1870 returns as *improved* 2,289,072 acres, leaving unimproved 3,650,128 acres. Deduct from this latter amount 650,122 acres, as unproductive and occupied by ponds, lakes, rivers, mountain summits and other barren areas, and there remains 3,000,000 of acres in forest.

Not less than five of the Maples: (1) *Red Maple* (Acer rubrum); (2) the *White Maple* (A. diascarpum); (3) the *Rock Maple* (A. saccharinum); (4) the *Striped Maple* (A. Pennsylvanicum); (5) the *Black Sugar Maple* (A. nigrum).

Two certainly of the Ash: (1) the *White Ash* (Fraxinus acuminata); (2) the *Black or Brown Ash* (F. sambucifolia).

Five at least of the Birch: (1) *Black Birch* (Betula linta); (2) the *Canoe Birch* (B. papyracea); (3) *White Birch* (B. populifolia); (4) the *Yellow Birch* (B. excelsa); (5) the *Red Birch* (B. nigra).

One of the Beech: (Fagus sylvatica).

One of the Hemlock: (Abies Canadensis).

Two of the Spruce: (1) the *Black or Double Spruce* (Abies nigra); (2) the *White or Single Spruce* (A. alba).

One of the Hackmatack: (Sarix Americana).

Two of the Cedar: (1) *White Cedar* (Cupressus thyoides); (2) the *Red Cedar* (Juniperus Virginiana).

Two of the Elm: (1) the *American Elm* (Ulmus Americana); (2) the *Slippery Elm* (Ulmus fulva).

One of the Tripelo or Hornbeam: (Nyssa multiflora).

Three of the Poplar: The *Large Poplar* (Populus grandidentata; (2) the *American Aspen* (P. tremulifirmis); (3) the *Balm of Gilead* (P. candicus).

One of the Basswood: (Tilia Americana).

Besides, there might be presented a long list of others, some of them very common and others less so, but all highly esteemed for building or manufacturing purposes. The precise number of the different species, a careful examination only of our woods, can determine, but it will exceed, without doubt, an hundred.

Among the agricultural products of this State, in 1870, those of the forest exceeded in value, every other except hay and slaughtered cattle, amounting to $2,351,612, or, about eleven per cent. of the entire aggregate of our farm productions.

Lumber and wood bring ready cash in the market and always have. In good old Provincial times, when the inhabitants of New Hampshire had little money, boards and pipe staves were a legal tender for taxes, and their value was fixed by statute. Unlike the hay and other crops we raise, these may be sold and consumed off the farm, without impoverishing it. And, but for the dividend made him every winter by his wood and timber lands, many a farmer would find it difficult to pay his store bills and his taxes, particularly, if he expends as much for foreign corn and flour as many are now doing, and which might and ought to be produced at home.

Mr. George B. Emerson says, in his report upon the trees and shrubs of Massachusetts, published in 1846, that no less than sixty-six of the trades and manufactories of that State were dependent, wholly or in part, for their working material, upon the forests. This remark, true there twenty-seven years ago, is doubtless true, and perhaps more than true, in New Hampshire to day.

Our forests are important too for other reasons. They perform an invaluable office in sheltering the pastures and cultivated fields from the cold and oftentimes violent winds, that would otherwise do serious injury to their herbage and other crops. And, where these are wanting, our best agricultural writers have repeatedly urged the planting of tree belts for this very purpose.

And then, too, the forests exert an important influence upon our climate, moderating the extremes of heat and cold, rendering our summers cooler and our winters more tolerable than they would otherwise be.

They also intercept the clouds which the east winds bear westward from the ocean and wring from them the moisture with which they are freighted, precipitating it in rains upon the spongy earth beneath, to be there protected from evaporation and held in reserve until wanted by the myriad springs and streamlets that unite and form the river system of the State.

Sweep from our mountains and hillsides and plains, the trees that now robe them in verdure and they would, ere long, become barren, and to barrenness would soon succeed a desolation as awful as that of the Sahara. The rivers, that sweep now in beauty through our meadows and afford motive power to those great interests that build up our largest cities and most thriving villages; these rivers would forsake their channels, except at intervals, when they returned as mountain torrents, bearing inundation and destruction to all they met; going forth in madness, on errands of violence which no human power could restrain; a curse to the land instead of a blessing; an Alaric instead of a messenger of beneficence.

But I need urge no further the importance of this great branch of our agriculture. It is as apparent as it is real.

DIMINUTION OF OUR FORESTS.

Allow me now to ask, what is being done for the improvement or preservation even of this magnificent heritage upon which "we are reaping where we have not sown, and gathering where we have not strewed?" Nothing, almost literally nothing. We are doing less than our forefathers did, more than two hundred years ago, when New Hampshire was a Province under the Stuarts; for, as early as 1640, only two years after the settlement of that town, the inhabitants of Exeter regulated the cutting of oak timber by a general order. And, twenty-eight years afterwards, the falling of all pine trees fit for masts, within three miles of the meeting-house of this same town, was forbidden by statute. Some forty years later still (1708) an act passed the Provincial Assembly to prevent the cutting of all mast trees on ungranted land by a penalty of £100 sterling. New Hampshire had too, in those days, a Surveyor-General of forests, and woe be to a man daring to fall a pine, upon which he had blazed the royal mark of the "broad arrow."

In many European countries, laws analagous to these, have long been in force and promoted greatly the protection and preservation of their forests.

About four years ago, Kansas, in order to encourage the planting of forests, made provision, by statute, for the payment of a bounty of two dollars per acre, per annum, for a period of twenty-five years, amounting in the aggregate to fifty dollars per acre, on all forests planted and maintained in that State.

Missouri has since followed this example and agricultural organizations in Massachusetts, New York, Illinois and California have also offered bounties for the promotion of forest culture in their several States. Indeed there is reason to hope from recent advices that, before the close of its present session, Congress will adopt measures for the preservation of a portion at least of the timber now standing upon the public lands.

But in our own State no steps have yet been taken in this direction, and the rapid destruction of the forests is painfully apparent everywhere. Large quantities of lumber, both manufactured and in the rough, are being exported continually. Some five or six millions pass down the Merrimack in the log every year; more also goes down the Androscoggin and the Saco; much is sent away upon the cars in boards and dimension timber. Our numerous manufacturing establishments of furniture, carriages, agricultural implements, and other articles of wood, consume large quantities, the State Prison alone converting over 2,000,000 feet into bedsteads every year.

The railroads are also large consumers of both timber and wood. Those centering at Concord, with their branches, use annually of the latter, about 72,000 cords at their shops and on their locomotives. If these afford a fair index of the amount required by the other lines, the aggregate railroad consumption must be 123,000 cords. Assuming the lands furnishing this to yield an average of thirty cords an acre, forty-one hundred acres must be swept clean, every twelve months, to meet this demand; a very large surface, when it is considered that all this is necessarily taken from the belts of land bordering upon the road, and not exceeding six or eight miles in width.

These same roads also renew their sleepers once in about seven years and a half, and reckoning 2,300 to a mile, must have 250,000 new ones each year to maintain their tracks in good condition. They have too, some fifteen hundred miles of fence, which annually requires for its reconstruction and repairs, more than two millions of feet of boards and posts.

When, to such amounts as these are added those required for buildings, farm fences, bridges, fuel, etc., we can easily account for the rapid destruction of our forests. Much of it, however, is thoughtless, unwise and wanton. An observing writer has very truly said that "the cunning foresight of the Yankee seems to desert him when he takes the axe in hand." It requires no prophet to divine the sad consequences of such a course. Wood will soon become scarce in many sections, and timber in all. We have already exhausted, to a very great extent, our first class pine lumber, and are sending to Maine, Michigan, and Canada for much that we now use, and even these sources of supply will not continue always. Mr. J. F. Joy, the Vanderbilt of Michigan, has recently stated that the eastern shore of Lake Michigan sends to market 350,000,000 feet of lumber annually. Another locality in that same State is expecting to cut and export 200,000,000 feet this very winter. It also appears by a statement in the last report of the U. S. Department of Agriculture, that Wisconsin and the upper Peninsula of Michigan are annually exporting the enormous quantity of 1,750,000,000 feet, and that, should this exportation continue unabated, the lumber of these sections will be exhausted in twelve years. As the supply diminishes, prices, as a matter of course, proportionately advance. Thirty-five years ago, the best of hard wood could be bought in Concord market for two dollars a cord. It is now worth seven or eight. I have in my mind an eighty foot barn, the white pine boarding and hard pine frame of which were furnished in 1831, for seven dollars a thousand. A similar schedule of lumber of the same quality would now cost three times as much, and this rise is not confined to any one, or to a few localities. It may be observed everywhere, varying indeed in amount, from Indian Stream to Massachusetts line; the inevitable result of an increased demand accompanied by a diminished supply.

If our forests fail, our various industries that draw from them the raw materials of their manufactures must also fail, and the cities and towns, and villages, to which these impart vitality, must sink to insignificance, and with them the local markets that encourage our agriculture, and make it remunerative.

THE REMEDY.

Now, what can we do to avert the dangers that impend, for I hold that we cannot afford much longer to do nothing? It is said that a fashionable little lady, who had never had a serious thought in all her life, once walked up to the side of the cynical, but sensible Leighton, as he sat upon the piazza of his hotel at the Shoals, and in lisping articulation inquired of him what he could possibly find to do on that lone island in winter. Surveying for an instant, with a glance of compassionate contempt, the fluttering mass of flounces that stood expectant before him, he laconically replied, "I think." And the first thing for us to do, is to collect together such facts as we can, bearing upon this great interest, and ponder them with a seriousness commensurate with their importance, for the disaster that threatens comes mostly of our thoughtlessness.

And nothing would help us more in coming to right conclusions than a thorough survey of all our forests, making known to us their varying characters, condition, and situation. It would aid immensely any intelligent examination of the subject. Some of the wisest European governments secured such surveys long ago, and upon them have based much of their forest legislation. Indeed, our legislature could not do a wiser thing than to order such a survey. Forestry should, and doubtless will, ere long, be taught in our Agricultural College. France, Bavaria and Prussia, have each instituted special schools, in which men are trained in the scientific and economical management of timber lands. The former had, before the late war, 2,300,000 acres of forests, less in quantity than ours, but which yielded an annual income of $8,700,000, nearly four times the amount afforded by the wood and timber lands of New Hampshire.

This subject should be discussed at our agricultural meetings and by our agricultural papers, just as all other branches of farming are discussed. But we need, as introductory to these discussions, accurate statistics relating to the subject. These would afford safe suggestions and lead to the institution of such experiments as the proper settlement of our forest policy demands. We need to know what varieties of trees we now have in our woods; the different rates of their increase, and under what conditions they grow the fastest; what soils are most favorable to the production of each, and to what uses they are best adapted; at what ages the different species of trees should be cut, and, in short, all other facts that will indicate to us the best methods of managing growing wood and timber.

We talk about wood and timber lands. In the older countries which were driven years ago to the contemplation of this subject, we hear mostly of timber lands. The raising of timber is the end sought. Wood, though economically cared for, is an incident only, and regarded as of comparatively small importance. Our future experience will doubtless develop a similar sentiment, and the sooner we get to appreciate the difference in value between a timber lot and a wood lot, the sooner we shall approach a true policy as to the management of this great interest. No prices we have yet reached will warrant the cutting and transportation of ordinary mixed wood more than five or six miles to a market. The wood purchased for the Concord Railroad, during the last six years, has cost an average price per cord of three dollars and seventy-five cents, and hardly any of it has been drawn a distance of more than three or four miles. Standing mixed wood, therefore, eight miles from a market, has no value worth mentioning.

But it is not so with timber. This will pay transportation for almost any distance. Much of the hard wood lumber used in the manufacture of bedsteads at our State Prison nets its owners four and five dollars per thousand on the stump, while the same trees, cut into wood, would not be of sufficient value to pay for the cutting. I have in my mind a growth of white pine trees sold some two years ago for ten dollars per thousand, standing. To cut into wood they were worth but about one dollar and a half a thousand.

While it will not be found profitable, as a general thing, to raise wood, it will almost always pay to raise timber on low-priced land, adapted to its growth. To this therefore, we should chiefly look.

Under some circumstances, however, wood is the most profitable crop. A growth of this, being produced in one-half or one-third of the time required for the maturing of timber, two or three crops of the former may be had to one of the latter; so that, in localities where low-priced lands are found, and wood commands a high price, it will yield a better profit than timber, particularly if the item of interest be introduced to the calculation.

But such cases are exceptional. Timber, however, is remunerative in all localities, whether on the swells of Rockingham, or the hills of Cheshire, or the mountain sides of Coos. Our lumber men seek it everywhere. They are cutting it to-day on the slopes of Kearsarge. Millions will be fallen this winter on the remotest tributaries of the Merrimack, the Saco and the Androscoggin. The haunts of the bear will be invaded, and the wilds of the Magalloway enlivened by the shout of the teamster and the ring of the axe. What matters the remoteness of the locality, when our maddest mountain torrents can be bridled for its transport, and the locomotive rushes through all sections of the State, not only disturbing the quiet of our valleys, but sounding the yell of its whistle upon our highest mountain peak, and literally mingling the defiant breath of its nostrils with the vapor of the clouds.

It is for the highest interest of every country to have a portion of its area in forest. What that portion shall be, depends upon the soil, location and other varying circumstances attaching to any particular country. In New Hampshire, as we have already remarked, about one-half the surface is in wood and timber. Considering the large amount of land we have that is unprofitable for tillage, or even pasturage, this is none too much. Indeed it had better be more than less, and instead of lamenting as we often do, the abandonment of hard farms, we should rather rejoice that they are to be devoted to a use that will render them more productive.

It is only to be regretted that means cannot profitably be taken to cover them with trees in a shorter time than unaided nature requires for the work.

MANUFACTURE OF FOREST PRODUCTS AT HOME.

The cheapest as well as the most convenient way of obtaining the wood and timber we need is to raise it. We avoid thereby the outlays requisite for its importation, and increase to that extent the wealth of the State.

And next to the folly of importing lumber is that of sending it abroad in a rough state, thereby realizing to ourselves but a small part of the value it bears when manufactured.

The difference between a given amount of lumber in the rough and in the manufactured state, is much greater than is commonly supposed. The President of the New Hampshire Board of Agriculture handed me, a few days since, a statement carefully prepared by himself, of the value at his mill, of a cord of white pine wood and also of the mackerel kits subsequently made from the same; that of the former being four dollars and seventy-five cents, and that of the latter twenty-five dollars and twenty cents,—a gain to the State of twenty dollars and forty-five cents above what would have accrued to it had the wood been exported before its manufacture; and more, even, as this would have been worth less for exportation than the price affixed to it.

From another statement, similarly prepared by a gentleman extensively engaged in the manufacture of furniture, it appears that a thousand of the lumber used for that purpose is worth fifteen dollars in the plank at the mill, where it is sawed; when converted to furniture and ready for market it is worth ($75.60) seventy-five dollars and sixty cents, nearly the entire difference of sixty dollars and sixty cents on every thousand, being saved to New Hampshire by its manufacture at home, amounting in the course of a single year to more than a hundred thousand dollars, ($106,260.00.)

FORESTS IMPROVE THE SOIL.

A forest growth, instead of impoverishing a soil, improves it. It derives a considerable part of its support from the atmosphere, and supplies to the ground an annual dressing of leaves, more than equal to what it has extracted from it. Hence, by this means alone, exhausted fields may, in a course of years, be restored to fertility. Several of the Dukes of Athol, in Scotland, have planted extensive tracts of their poorest lands with larch trees. From these plantations they have not only derived lucrative returns in timber, but the lands thus treated, have been lifted from absolute barrenness to a fair degree of fertility.

PROFITABLENESS OF OUR FORESTS.

Does some one ask, what interest will a forest return upon its cost? A question involving so many and so various conditions, cannot easily be answered with a definiteness at all satisfactory. In part answer, however, I would say that, the lot of pine timber to which I have previously alluded, as having been sold, was a second growth and had been standing not far from eighty-five years, on a piece of very rocky, moist, hard-pan soil, sloping to the northwest. No care had ever been bestowed upon it, and it had grown unevenly, being much too thick in some spots, and too thin in others. At the time of sale, the growth was supposed, from careful estimates, to average twenty-two and a half thousand of timber and ten cords of wood to the acre. The price received for it was two hundred and thirty-five dollars an acre. Timber and wood had from time to time been previously cut upon it in sufficient amounts to offset its taxes. What, then, could a person have afforded to pay for it eighty-five years ago, to realize six per cent. simple interest on his investment? About thirty-eight dollars and fifty-two cents according to my computation, or one dollar and seventy-five cents if compound interest was demanded. Had it been properly cared for during its growth, the timber would have been of better quality, and might, doubtless, have attained the size it did, in three-fourths of this time. In that case it would have had an original value per acre of forty-eight dollars and fifty cents or five dollars and eighty-one cents, according to the rate of interest, simple or compound, required.

A wood lot, on a good soil and having a favorable exposure, may generally be expected to yield some thirty-five cords of mixed wood per acre, in thirty-six years. If this be worth one dollar a cord, upon the stump, it will pay six per cent. compound interest, during that time, on an original outlay of about four dollars and thirty-seven and a half cents an acre. Some wood grows much faster than this, yielding twenty cords in as many years, and forests of clump birch, in favorable locations, are occasionally seen-which can be profitably cut, oftener than once in twenty years.

GROWTH OF TIMBER.

The wood and timber of our forests, when left to itself grow less rapidly than is often supposed. I found, some years since, by counting the rings and measuring the buts of forty white pine logs, averaging about fifty feet in length, taken from various localities in the vicinity of Concord, that their average diameter was twenty-two and eighty-two one hundredth (22.82) inches, their average age, eighty-six and seventy-six one-hundredth (86.76) years, and their average contents three hundred and sixty three feet (363), showing an average growth of four and two-tenths (4.2) feet a year, board measure.

A similar examination of twenty chestnut logs, averaging thirty feet in length, showed their average diameter to be twenty-one and four-tenths (21.4) inches, their average age seventy-four (74) years, and their average contents two hundred and ninety-six feet, having increased at an average rate of four feet a year.

Twenty red oak logs of an average length of thirty feet, and an average diameter of eighteen and two-tenths (18.2) inches, had an average age of seventy and one-tenth (70.1) years, and contained on an average, two hundred and fifty-three feet, having grown at the rate of three and six-tenths (3.6) feet, each year.

Five hemlock logs averaging thirty-five feet in length, and seventeen and two-tenth (17.2) inches in diameter, had an average age of seventy-seven years, and an average measurement of two hundred and seventy-one (271) feet, having increased at the rate of three and a half feet a year.

Now, gentlemen, these are not encouraging figures upon which to base an after-dinner speech in glorification of our forests. But we can improve them, if we will set about it, and accelerate their growth as certainly, as, in enlightened animal husbandry, we can now secure as much beef, on an animal two or three years old, as we formerly did, on one four years old. In this, as in every other business, we want early returns, that will enable the profits to outrun the interest, which like the old Scotch laird's tree, grows "while ye're sleeping."

And not only earlier, but greater returns. Every good farmer well understands that it is more profitable to raise fifty bushels of corn to an acre, than twenty-five; the latter hardly paying its cost, while the former affords a fair profit. We don't apply to our forests the careful consideration which we bestow upon our fields. How many farmers there are who would refuse to sell a neighbor a bushel of corn, without measuring and even streaking it, but would be perfectly willing to sell to a stranger, they had never seen, an hundred acres of wood or timber, and guess at the quantity. That very philosophic gentleman, Mr. Tristram Shandy, gravely informs us that "the ancient Goths had all of them a wise custom of debating everything of importance to their state twice; once drunk and once sober." We shall do well to get a hint from these old barbarians and revolve and debate this great interest of our agriculture, not only twice, but thrice twice, and every time sober.

Yes, gentlemen, we need quicker and greater returns from our woodlands; and they are not beyond our reach. We can have them, if we will. How, do you ask? By adopting and pursuing a better system of management.

MANAGEMENT OF OUR FORESTS.

First. If any portion of a forest is wet, either from springs or stagnant water, it should, if practicable, be drained. It is in vain to expect satisfactory results from any crop on wet land.

Second. We should raise, as far as possible, either wood or timber, but not both indiscriminately. The former needs one kind of treatment and the latter another. The wood will crowd upon the timber and impede its growth, while the timber will overshadow the wood. In illustration of this fact, I see daily, when at home, two elms, both of which were set out on the same day more than a hundred years ago, for shade trees. The first, having had ample space in which to grow, has developed a magnificent top, and, at three feet from the ground, its trunk has a circumference of sixteen feet and ten inches. The second having been crowded by neighboring trees has a very small and imperfect top and measures at the same distance from the ground but nine feet and four inches, lagging behind the first, seven feet and six inches.

Third. Generally, a forest devoted to wood, had best be kept to itself until its trees are fit to be cut, when they should all be removed as fast as the ground is passed over. The old idea of taking out the least promising trees is, pretty generally, discountenanced by our most intelligent wood-growers. Better results are attained by cutting clean. A lot of thirty-five acres, on land maturing a satisfactory crop in as many years, will, when once properly started, yield annually an acre of wood for all time to come. By the time the last acre is cut off, for the first time, the first acre will be ready to be cut off a second time. A wood lot thus managed, is like the cruise of oil daily drawn from by the widow of Zarephath, constant in its supply and unfailing.

Fourth. But a timber lot calls for a different treatment. Here, besides rapid growth, long, smooth trunks and as few limbs as possible, are sought. To attain these ends, the growth, particularly if an evergreen one, should be left quite thick in its infancy. The trees will crowd upon one another somewhat, and not increase as fast as if they stood farther apart, but they will stretch continually upward and the lower limbs will die and fall off. As the tops thicken and begin seriously to exclude the sun and air, the lot should be thinned, care being taken to remove such trees as will leave those remaining scattered as evenly as possible over the ground. In a few years the tops will again thicken, more limbs will die and a second thinning be called for, to be repeated, every ten or fifteen years, until maturity. If judiciously done, on ground of fair productiveness, the three objects sought will be attained, viz: Rapidity of growth, and as large trees in sixty years, as nature unaided or improperly interfered with, would have produced in seventy-five; length of trunk, of great importance as affecting the quantity of timber; and smoothness of trunk, of no less consequence as influencing its quality.

On a lot thus treated, the trees will stand at pretty even distances from one another as the corn does in a corn field. And with about the same propriety, might this be sown broadcast and its stalks left to grow promiscuously, as to leave timber to grow thus.

Twenty thousand of pine timber to the acre is esteemed a good crop, but we ought to raise at least twice as much. By such a disposition of the trees that each shall occupy one square rod of ground and allowing them to stand until they average two hundred feet to a tree we may secure a crop of thirty-two thousand feet to the acre. If, at this time, every other one is removed, or sixteen thousand feet, and the remainder left standing, each tree on two square rods, until their size is doubled, the crop will again amount to thirty-two thousand per acre, the value of which added to that of sixteen thousand previously removed, enlarged by the accumulated interest thereon, very far exceeds any returns we now realize.

Forty-eight thousand of pine timber to an acre is not an impossible crop. It is certainly a pleasant one to anticipate. I am aware that it may be urged that, he who plants it cannot hope to live long enough to gather it. True, but do those that buy the new five per cent bonds of the Government feel quite sure of living to their maturity? The bond, however, will bring to its holder its value any day, and so will a good wood and timber lot.

Fifth. The age at which trees attain a fair degree of maturity, depends much upon their variety, the soil they occupy, the exposure to which they are subjected and the culture they receive.

As a general thing, unless injured by some means, or in the way, a tree should not be cut until ripe. Sapling lumber has not the density or firmness imparted by maturity, is weak and liable to quick decay upon exposure to the weather. Age consolidates the sap into heart wood, and in a tree of good size, the proportion of the latter to the former is much greater than in a small one.

The time of cutting, however, should be governed by the use to be made of the lumber cut, as it will be often found more profitable to cut fast growing saplings, such as white pines, wanted for staves, or small chestnuts for posts, before their maturity, than to keep them for larger timber.

Trees oftentimes continue to grow vigorously to great ages. I have ever been familiar with five elms, standing upon the oldest street of Concord, which were transplanted from the interval to the places they now occupy, on the second day of May, 1764. They are all yet flourishing and in vigorous health. The largest had a circumference of sixteen feet, at three feet from the ground, fifteen years ago. To-day, it measures sixteen feet and ten inches.

The hand of him (1) who planted these veteran elms has long mouldered in the dust, but they "still live" to extend their wide arms in benediction over his descendants to the fifth generation.

(1) Rev. Timothy Walker.

OUR FORESTS. 17

Through all periods of our country's history, from the bloody days when our fathers, spurning the hated name of rebel, with which an unjust government sought to stigmatize them, proved themselves patriots and American citizens; down to the bloodier days of our generation, these stalwart trees have stood, mute witnesses of the great march of events, reminding the living of the virtues of the dead, and gathering about them the associations of each passing age, that they may transmit them to the future. Their circumferences taken at three different times in 1856, 1864 and 1871, were as follows, viz:

TABLE,

Showing the increase in the Circumference of uncut Trees in Concord.

	1856.		1864.		1871.		Increase in eight years.		Increase in fifteen years.	
	three ft. from ground.	six feet from ground.	three ft. from ground.	six feet from ground.	three ft. from ground.	six feet from ground.	three ft. from ground.	six feet from ground.	three ft. from ground.	six feet from ground.
	ft. in.	ft. in.	ft. in.	ft. in.	ft. in.	ft. in.	inches.	inches.	inches.	inches.
South one............	16 0	14 0	16 4	14 10	16 10	15 8	4	10	10	15
Next North..........	12 9	12 3	13 5	12 10	14 1	13 5	8	7	16	14
Next North of that..	9 0	9 3	9 2	9 4	9 4	9 6	2	1	4	3
Next North of that..	13 0	12 0	13 2	12 3	13 3	12 7	2	3	3	7
On opposite side of street..	12 9	12 2	13 6	13 0	14 4	13 5	9	10	19	15

But these trees are children compared with many, of whose ages we have authentic records. The old Elm on Boston common was more than a hundred years old at the time of the Revolution. There was, not many years since, and is perhaps even now, a Linden tree in Fryeburg, Switzerland, which was planted sixteen years before the discovery of this continent by Columbus. Struth, in his Sylva Brittanica, mentions a tree which was of notable size in the reign of Stephen, who ascended the English throne in 1137. Some of the Cypress trees of Mexico are of incredible ages, the great one at Atlisco being over twenty-four hundred years old.

Sixth. I doubt if we have yet reached a point, here in New Hampshire, at which it is profitable to attempt very much in the way of planting forest trees, and so long as their seeds are left to nature's sowing we can control but partially the varieties to be produced on a given lot. But, we may do this to some extent by an early removal of those not wanted and by keeping those that are. So far as that control can be exercised it should be, and those only left to stand to whose growth the soil is well adapted. The diluvial sands of this valley are not favorable to the production of deciduous trees, but the pitch-pine prefers them to any other; and where oak and the rock maple would nearly or quite starve, the spruce and the hemlock will live luxuriously.

The summary, gentlemen, of the whole matter is this, viz:

(1) We have in our forests a magnificent heritage.

(2) We are destroying them with a recklessness and rapidity that is alarming.

(3) We are drifting towards a timber famine that diminished consumption or better treatment only can avert.

(4) Intelligently and systematically managed, our forests will yield annually profitable returns, not only to our own but to all succeeding generations.

No branch of husbandry furnishes more agreeable occupation than forest culture. It affords to the farmer pleasant diversion from the protracted labors of the field and employment for long winters that without it might prove monotonous.

There is, too, an interest attaching to the forests which the open fields do not afford. Their presence fascinates and enchants us. By subtle influences they seize upon our feelings ere we are aware and for all our varying moods afford their ready sympathies.

What better accords with our gayest hours than the resplendent robes of bright October woods, blazing in light and carpeted in colors richer by far than Persia's looms afford? How grateful in midsummer to flee for a while the oppressive heat and stroll in the cool of the trees whose tall trunks and o'er-arching branches first suggested the towering columns and lofty vaults of the cathedral! How grateful, in our serious mood, the deep shades of the forest, its solitude and its silence, disturbed only by the sweet voice of the birds, or the splash of the waterfall or the grand old anthem played by the wind in the coronals of high trunks which stand like vast organ pipes on every side around—imposing anthems, which, from creation's dawn have sounded and awed the soul of man to thoughts of its Creator and to prayer.

ABRONIA UMBELLATA.

Printed by Libri Plureos GmbH in Hamburg, Germany